Rethinking Evangelism:
Delivering the Gospel Outside the Box

Shawn Patrick Williams, D.D.

Greenwood, South Carolina

Copyright © 2014 Shawn Patrick Williams
All rights reserved.
ISBN: 10 1496137655
ISBN: 13 9781496137654
Printed by Warrior Nations Publications
        PO Box 2352
        Greenwood, South Carolina 29646
        (864) 227-0508

All rights reserved solely by the author. The author guarantees all contents are original and do not infringe upon the legal rights of any other person or work. No portion of this book may be reproduced, stored in a retrieval system, or transmitted in any form or by any means—electronic, mechanical, photocopy, recording, or any other—except for brief quotations in printed reviews, without the prior written permission of the author. The views expressed in this book are not necessarily those of the publisher.

All scripture quotations, unless otherwise indicated, are taken from THE HOLY BIBLE, NEW INTERNATIONAL VERSION®, NIV®
Copyright © 1973, 1978, 1984, 2011 by Biblica, Inc.™
Used by permission. All rights reserved worldwide.
Scripture marked NKJV are taken from the New King James Version®.
Copyright © 1982 by Thomas Nelson, Inc. Used by permission. All rights reserved.
Scripture marked KJV are taken from the King James Version.
The KJV is public domain in the United States.
Scripture is taken from GOD'S WORD®, © 1995 God's Word to the Nations. Used by permission of Baker Publishing Group.

warrior nations
PUBLICATIONS

"Giving Voice to the Remnant"

warriornationspublications.com

Shawn Patrick Williams

DEDICATION

As I was thinking about this project and contemplating who this book should be dedicated to, if anyone at all, I thought about who had been instrumental in helping Warrior Nations over the years to carry out the Great Commission. I thought about teachers, preachers, and prophets who had impacted my life. I thought about all the influential people I had met in the vast travels of this ministry and I quickly came to the undeniable decision of who that person was.

I want to dedicate <u>Rethinking Evangelism: Delivering the Gospel Outside the Box</u> to all of the Warrior Nations' Remnant Partners who have been faithful every month to support the mission God has commissioned us to. I think about all the times we have been out preaching the Gospel around the World, and able to be there because of all those who have stood with us through the years. Despite a radical ministry name and "out of the box" message, you have been there. My family and this ministry are forever grateful for your prayers, support, and love that have impacted so many.

And to my greatest partner of all, Christy. We are still here doing what God called us to do. Thank you for pushing me to be a better minister of the Gospel!

TABLE OF CONTENTS

	Dedication	v
1	Personal Evangelism	1
2	How To Prepare Your Testimony	9
3	Post-Modern Evangelism	13
4	Power Evangelism	17
5	Corporate Evangelism: Phase One	21
6	Corporate Evangelism: Phase Two	27
7	Corporate Evangelism: Phase Three	31
8	Kingdom Synergy	35
9	The Office of an Evangelist	39
10	The Secret to Evangelism	43
11	Appendix	45

"Warrior Nations is one of the leading 'last days' evangelistic ministries God is using to impact America and the nations."

-Dorothy Spaulding, *Watchmen Broadcasting Network, Augusta, GA*

PERSONAL EVANGELISM

My Testimony

It was a night I'll never forget! I strolled on an empty beach with the waves crashing down on the East coast shore. The moon was the only light; however, it was unusually bright this night. It seemed like I walked for miles without seeing a soul – and I was looking. I had just left The Pier, which is a bar on Jax Beach in Jacksonville, FL. It was my eighteenth birthday. I was alone, living on the streets, drunk, and miles away from what I used to call home. I was angry, scared, hurt, confused, depressed, and deceived, all at once.

It was unusually cold for an August summer night, but then again so was my heart. "God, why have you let this happen to me? Why have you done this to my life? If you are so powerful, why can't you do anything for me? If this is Jesus, I don't want you! Can you hear me God? Are you listening to me?" No thunder, no fireworks, no help, and no God. "That's what I thought, nothing!"

The clouds seemed to move across the sky quickly darkening the light that I once had and then darkness filled my head. Then again, darkness had been filling my head for years, slowly and subtly without notice, gradually bringing me to this place where I now stood. "Satan, if you are real, I call upon you."

That night was the beginning of the worst and most cursed seven years of my life. Over the years, I plunged into drug addiction, greed, paranoia, panic attacks, occultism, sexual bondage, rage, and depression. I was always seeking, but never finding. I was around everyone, but always alone. I had even come to the point of wanting to end my own life. How could I have gotten so far gone, so far away from my Christian upbringing? I mean, I was raised in a Christian family and we went to church several times a week. How could I have gotten so far away from the God of my youth?

I often ask myself that question. What was it that caused my perception of life and my view of God to become so twisted that I would reject Him and embrace Satan? Was it the compromises that I had made with my choices of music or movies? Was it that one sip or that just one hit that turned into just one more line? Did I barter my soul away in a thousand little compromises long before I actually "sold" it?

Where did it all start? Who or what did it all start with? Was it the people I chose to be around, the places I chose to go, or was it the latest trend I chose to follow? All these questions have surfaced as I have looked back on that night on August 16, 1991.

Have you ever had a moment in your life when you stopped, looked around and thought, "How in the world did I get here?" On August 16, 1998, I looked around and found myself starring into the eyes of leaders in the Church of Satan and the Santeria cult. It was exactly seven years to the hour from the night I made a vow to Satan on Jax beach in Florida. Here I was surrounded by darkness, and for the first time in that seven-year period I could see what my life had become and where it was going.

Soon after that night on Jax Beach in 1991, I found a renewed and intense ambition in dealing drugs. I moved in with a group that was involved in Wicca and the New Age movement. I was selling drugs to everybody I could. Some of the people were heavily involved in witchcraft. Some were into the criminal organizations like the Mexican Mafia and Dixie Mafia; others were in the Hell's Angels and some were into bands, such as 311 and Widespread Panic.

During these years of darkness, I experienced some very crazy things as I became closer to some of these people involved in witchcraft. I went from living on the streets of Atlanta, GA, to opening a bar in South Carolina. When I was in Atlanta, I went to all the music festivals, raves and clubs to sell drugs at the events. I was mentored in the bar business by a Reverend in the Church of Satan and a High Priest in the Santeria cult. These people took me in and were grooming me for this underground network they control. I can remember times when they would do rituals in the bar and release incantations (spells) over their bar and other businesses to be successful. I experienced two of my roommates becoming demonically possessed and questioning me on my views of sin. While living with them in a warehouse, the demonic oppression was so strong that, while under the influence of cocaine, I actually drank my own blood, and I did so without really knowing why I was doing it.

After five years of living this lifestyle, my brother asked me to help him establish a bar and grill in South Carolina. I wasn't exactly thrilled about leaving the fast-paced lifestyle of Atlanta, but I knew that I needed some change. Before I left, the Santeria priest released many incantations through spells, stones, herbs, and tarot cards over me, my brother, and the business we were about to open. For the next two years of my life, the bar and grill prospered, and so did the drug business. In the middle of all this success that I had longed for as a teenager came a very high price to pay. I had become very paranoid, greedy, and a miserable drug addict. I started snorting and shooting cocaine, and eating as many hits of ecstasy or acid as I could without overdosing. I did that on many occasions, and then I started to flirt with and even attempt suicide.

The more destructive and violent my behavior became, the greater my desire to become a member of this "elite" occult network. I realized that my ties to these people stemmed from that night on the beach in Florida. During this time, a demon spirit started revealing himself to me. The spirit began tempting me with ideas about ruling the underworld and the business through its demonic power.

Getting In or Getting Out

Around the same time, there were two very significant things that happened to me that caused me to question this dark path I had chosen. The first was one weekend I went up to the north Georgia mountains with an older leader in the Dixie Mafia to visit a trucking company they owned. They used this company as a front to transport drugs and launder money. Throughout the entire weekend, he kept giving me the introduction to his group trying to get me to work through them selling drugs. At the end of the weekend, one of his protégés took me outside during the day to show me something. As I stepped outside, this guy said something and extended his hand outward. Suddenly a blue lightning energy came shooting out of his fingertips.

At this point, I began to understand just how serious my situation had become. During this same time, my business mentor from the church of Satan kept showing me his red card and asking me if I was interested in becoming an ordained minister! The pressure was unbelievable and the temptation was reaching a peak. I knew something had to give. Either I was getting in or I was getting out, and it felt like in.

The Offer

On my 25th birthday, seven years to the night of my vow on the beach in Florida, I drove to Atlanta, GA to surprise my friends and celebrate my birthday. I was the one in for the big surprise on this particular night. When I arrived at the club, one of the largest rave clubs in Atlanta, all of my friends in this network were in the back office waiting for me. I told no one that I was traveling out of the state that night. My friends from all over the country just happened to be there that night.

Toward the end of the night my mentor walked me up into the disc jockey's booth to show me something. He pointed over the sea of people dancing and asked me to look at their new artwork. As I looked over the crowd, I saw a painting of a dark angel with its wings spread, and in the corner I saw a dark perverted outline of Jesus. Nobody else could see the painting unless they were standing in the booth. The dark Reverend turned around, looked me in the eyes, and with his arms wide open, made me an offer of partnership in his business and an opportunity to be a brother in this network.

At that very moment, he turned around with his arms wide open and looked me in the eyes. A voice spoke to me and said, "Heaven is real, Hell is real, and you have to make a choice." Suddenly it was as if light filled every fiber of my body. I became completely conscious of my spiritual state. The drugs and alcohol seemed to fade away and the conviction from the Holy Spirit was the only thing on my mind. At that very moment, I made a new vow, this time to God. I promised that if God would get me out of this situation, I would serve Him for the rest of my life. I spent the rest of the night listening to my mentor telling me his master plan of how we were going to become millionaires within six months to a year, but all I could think about was getting back to South Carolina and finding that old Bible that I had packed away years ago.

A New Start

In the middle of the darkest time of my life, the light of Jesus Christ shone through every satanic curse and stronghold in my life in an instant. I Peter 2:9 says, "But ye are a chosen generation, a royal priesthood, an holy nation, a peculiar people; that ye should shew forth the praises of him who hath called you out of darkness into his marvelous light."

It doesn't matter in what kind of darkness you have ever been involved; the light of Jesus Christ, through His shed blood, is more powerful. Our culture has many avenues in which occult doors can be opened in your life, but no demon spirit is more powerful than the blood of Jesus and the Holy Spirit of Jesus Christ, which lives in you after salvation.

That night, I left the rave club with my mentor and the other people there, who were involved in this occult network. They took me to a warehouse downtown. As we pulled up, there was a hatch door that led to the basement. The basement was constructed of bricks and located in the center was one large room surrounded by doors leading into other rooms.

On the walls in the center room were satanic symbols and writings in red. No one left the center room. My mentor stayed with me in the building telling me the details of his plan for the future. I was very scared, but I tried not to show any signs of fear.

Everybody in this room was involved in this network except the one friend I invited to come with us right before I left the club. I could tell my mentor was a little reluctant for my friend to come, but I knew that a blood sacrifice, or a ritual was the next step to do. During the course of the night my friend and I were able to quickly slip out of the warehouse and leave the downtown area.

I drove back to South Carolina the next day and for the first time in years my mind was clear and I could think clearly. I could hear and understand every demonic lyric to every song on my compact discs. I never recognized them before, but the Spirit of God, who is light, shined light into the dark areas of my life.

I started to read my Bible every time temptation would come to my mind. I was completely delivered from drug addiction, occult spells, sexual perversion, violence, anger, greed, and much more through the blood of Jesus, praying and fasting, and quoting the written Word of God.

The Calling

God is calling a generation out of the darkness into His marvelous light. God is no respecter of persons. If God can make a way of escape out of the darkness for me, He will do it for anyone. I don't care how impossible a situation may seem, God's light will expose and expel any darkness in your life.

I began to fast and pray for this network of people in Atlanta. For six to nine months it was pure spiritual warfare in my life. People entered into my home through astral projection and demons manifested to try to scare me and to stop my prayers, but I had light for the first time and no demon in Hell could take that away from me. I was sealed with the Spirit of Light for eternity.

After about a year, I began to be mentored by Billy Mayo. He is the evangelist who had a similar conversion and exposed occultism in rock music back in the late 80's and 90's through backward masking. This gave me a very powerful foundation to withstand darkness and understand evangelism.

In 2002, God gave me a vision of a generation of young men and women who were being raised up to start a spiritual revolution in America. It was an Army of Light, a warrior nation that God was forming out of the Body of Christ to combat and conquer the darkness that has robbed multiple generations from their destiny.

October of that same year, my wife and I started "Warrior Nations International Ministries, Inc." (also known as WNIM). It is a non-profit 501(c)(3) evangelistic outreach for the purpose of gathering these men and women from this dark culture and raising them up to be part of this warrior generation that is piercing and exposing the darkness of this American culture with the light of Jesus Christ.

WNIM has a core purpose of evangelism. We preach revival style meetings in churches. We organize prayer and worship services called "i3" in which we have seen the Holy Spirit work in mighty ways. We have preached meetings in over 20 different denominations. Our passion is souls! We hold evangelistic meetings called, "Beyond the Darkness" that expose cultural trends such as occult music, movies, and much more; however, the main purpose is to gather the harvest of souls into the Kingdom of God. We conduct meetings called, "Warring with the Word Spiritual Warfare Conferences" that are designed to equip this army with the weapons they need to win this war on darkness. These conferences are an extension of our first book called, <u>Warring with the Word.</u>

There is a God-ordained mandate in the spiritual realm for evangelism and revival. The Lord is preparing and empowering many people and ministries to answer His call. There is a war cry going out in the spirit. It is a call to arms, a call to battle this army of darkness with the unfailing power of the light of Jesus Christ.

God is calling an entire generation out of the dark pews of our churches, out of the dark alleys and the streets of America, out of the dark places of our culture, and into the marvelous army of light. There has never been a time like there is right now to take the gospel to world! Outside-the-box evangelism is what this world needs. According to a 2009 study, 33% of the people in the world confesses to be a Christian. In early 2013, the global population is more than 6.8 billion people. If only one third are believers in Jesus, that means more than 4.5 billion people are lost and going to Hell! Think about how many people you personally know that don't have a true relationship with Jesus. Ask yourself how many people you know that have never truly been born again.

You are the most important evangelism strategy Jesus has. The purpose of this book is to equip every believer with a firm understanding how to lead someone to Jesus, to understand the role of an evangelist, the different dynamics of evangelism, and to give fresh evangelism ideas for you to get Outside the box of the church. We pray this book inspires you to be witness in an unconventional way. No matter what you pull out of this book, my charge to you is simply this: just do it!

HOW TO PREPARE YOUR TESTIMONY

"And Jesus, walking by the sea of Galilee, saw two brethren, Simon called Peter, and Andrew his brother, casting a net into the sea: for they were fishers. And he saith unto them, Follow me, and I will make you fishers of men."
Matthew 4:18-19 KJV

"Jesus said to them, "Come, follow me! I will teach you how to catch people instead of fish."
Matthew 4:19 GW

When I moved from the city of Atlanta to rural South Carolina, I was blown away by country things. I was use to the city. I never went fishing, or walking through the woods, or anything thing much like that. I remember sitting in a field looking at how bright the stars were. In the city the night sky was pink all the time from the reflection of streetlights. Light pollution stole the innocence of the stars, so when I came to South Carolina, I loved just looking at the clear sky. It wasn't long before someone took me fishing. I learned pretty quickly that worms on a hook casting from the shore isn't really the best bait or position to catch a Bass. You are going to have a much better chance at getting a big old catfish, but not a bass. If you want a bass, you need to change your bait to a spinner, or a minnow, but not worms. Then you are going need to need to get on a boat or a pier. You want to get out in the water. Oh, and it all depends on how hot or cold the weather is that day.

I'm not a professional fisherman, obviously, but I know enough that all fish don't like the same bait! In the Gospel accounts, Jesus was dealing with professional fishermen. They knew all about fish'in. I can guarantee they knew they had to adjust their efforts and techniques to get the best results. I want to give some helpful tips that I pray will make your personal evangelism efforts bear fruit.

Your story is your testimony. Your testimony is nothing more than you sharing from your heart how Jesus has impacted your life. I have laid the foundation of our ministry simply telling my story. Think about what life was like before you were born again. Think about what your background was and how it affected your view of God. What was it that brought you to a place of making the choice to ask Jesus to be your Lord? How has your life been different since then? What are some of the stories that you have of your transition from the kingdom of darkness to the kingdom of light? All of these details are important because they help people understand your journey.

Share your story from your heart. This is not a numbers game or a platform to condemn the world in hate. I will never pull punches when talking about sin or Hell. When I do mention sin or Biblical morality, I make it clear to people that I'm not talking about them, but their choices. Hate the sin and love the sinner. You can quote the Romans road until you are blue in the face, but people must open up their heart to the Holy Spirit. Do not sound like a robot. People need real in this day and hour. Be real.

Develop good listening skills. Once I share my story, I will listen to the responses of the person. I can tell quickly what the next direction of the conversation will be. Once you ask someone, "If you died today, do you know where you will spend eternity?" you can usually hear details about their spiritual state. Simply listen.

If your bait isn't working, change it. Not everyone can relate to my experience dabbling in the occult, but a lot of people can relate to my time battling with religion. Or they can relate with my time battling with addiction. Maybe they can relate to my time battling with greed or porn. Street people want to hear about my time living on the streets. Business people want to hear about my time in business. Whenever I am talking to someone and I notice they have a similar situation to mine, that's what I will focus on. I do my best to find common ground with people. The Apostle Paul said that he became all things to all people that he might win some. Don't lie! That's "evange'lie'ing". Simply change your bait if the fish ain't biting.

Share your story often. Where ever you are becomes a mission field. Some call this contact evangelism. Whomever you come in contact with is a potential candidate to hear your story. Work, school, the gym, the store, and even church can be your mission field. Just do it- God will show you how faithful He is.

POST-MODERN EVANGELSIM

"Excuse me sir. Is this seat taken?", I said to a man that looked to be in his mid-twenties. He looked at me and shook his head, "No." "Thanks. Where are you from?" I asked. "From Frankfurt, Germany." He replied. I continued to tell them man where I was from and he asked what I was doing. I told him about some of the recent meetings in the Kabera slums in Nairobi. "Do you know Jesus Christ?" I asked the young German man, as we both sat in a coffee lounge in the Nairobi, Kenya airport waiting for our flight to Europe. "What? Do I know who Jesus was? Are you some kind of Imperialist radical Christian that wants to take something from me, or make me just like you? You're American right?", replied the hostile young European. "That's not at all what I mean. I have had an encounter with the risen Holy Spirit of Jesus Christ. He is alive and very well. I have never been the same and simply wanted to share my story with you." I carefully responded back. This man went on to let his guard down and listen to my testimony. He proceeded to explain to me the perspective of Christianity of a large growing number of European youth in what has become known as "Postmodern Christianity" in Europe.

...as an encounter that I so desperately needed to prepare me ...next 36 hours in Amsterdam, Holland. There, I embarked with... team member on the streets of one of the world's closest examples of a modern day Sodom and Gomorrah. The spiritual atmosphere was so cold. After witnessing to over seventy people on those historical streets and feeling the vibrations of wickedness from the gift of discernment of spirits, I began to understand just what my German friend was describing at the Nairobi coffee shop.

Postmodernism is a philosophical movement evolved in reaction to modernism, the tendency in contemporary culture to accept only objective truth and to be inherently suspicious towards a global cultural narrative or meta-narrative. Postmodernist thought is an intentional departure from the previously dominant modernist approaches. The term "postmodernism" comes from its critique of the "modernist" scientific mentality of objectivity and the progress associated with the Enlightenment.

Postmodernism postulates that many, if not all, apparent realities are only social constructs and are therefore subject to change. It emphasizes the role of language, power relations, and motivations in the formation of ideas and beliefs. In particular it attacks the use of sharp classifications such as male versus female, straight versus gay, white versus black, and imperial versus colonial; it holds realities to be plural and relative, and to be dependent on whom the interested parties are and of what their interests consist. It supports the belief that there is no absolute truth and that the way in which different people perceive the world is subject to change with society and time. Postmodernism has influenced many cultural fields, especially religion.

Over the centuries, the world and the Church have had many ideologies about the term and function of the Evangelist. Throughout the book of Acts, the foundation was beginning to be laid for all the saints to come in the years ahead. Somewhere from the birth of the church until the time Constantine ruled the Roman Empire, defining some of these functions in the body of Christ became very confusing because of the attempted adoption of the original church by the Roman Catholic church. In the 11th century the Christian Crusades began and evangelism model looked very different from the original New Testament model of the early church.

Think about it in terms of a postmodern view. The church went from a spontaneous organism based on love, selflessness and enduring persecution, into a Roman institutionalized organization and then was viewed as an army sent to spark genocide in the Middle East to the Muslims. Then five hundred years later, the Church kills a man named Martin Luther and some of its own for having postmodern ideas that sparked what was known as the Protestant Reformation. Then one hundred or so years after that a group of those came to a "new land" and forced the native people to believe the same way they did. Not too long after that they again committed genocide to the native people. Killing them and or enslaving them were legal in the new land. Now these same people are killing or enslaving Africans – and it's perfectly legal – but they are also sending "missionaries" to Africa in droves for an imperialistic indoctrination. But wait; now they have the most powerful army in the world and are trying to spread "Democracy" around the world by the same method of imperialistic hope with the same hidden agenda of selfish gain.

Listen to what Rabbi Rami Shapiro (a famous theologian and educator) said in the November/December issue of *Outreach Magazine*: "I'm open to the truth where I can find it – in Buddhism, Christianity, Islam, in science and art." This was an example of a postmodern Rabbi's view of spirituality.

I firmly believe that there has always been a remnant of God's people keeping the purity of the purpose of the church alive, but looking over the centuries and defining a general understanding of how the church has become what it is from where it came, can be a bit confusing. Well, my point is that our worldview has distorted a true biblical understanding of the church and the evangelism function. Unfortunately, 2000 years later, the modern church is still trying to understand what the apostle Paul was talking about in the letter to Ephesus about different gifts sent to the Church for the development of the Church. No matter how much our society changes, God plan for the church is still the same. The problem comes in when you worship the mission more than you worship the Messiah. Then you miss the very essence of evangelism seeing people fall in love with Jesus!

"And he gave some, apostles; and some, prophets; and some, evangelists; and some, pastors and teachers; For the perfecting of the saints, for the work of the ministry, for the edifying of the body of Christ."
Ephesians 4:11-13

An evangelist is "a preacher of the gospel." The best advice I have ever heard for reaching a group of foreign people was by Billy Graham. "When I go into a nation I find a connection with the people I am speaking to. I find a common denominator between them and Jesus Christ." The apostle Paul said that he would become "all things to all people" that he might win some. I believe the core of evangelism is simply telling people the good news of what Jesus has done in your life and looking for culturally relevant ways to express that message to people without compromising the message.

POWER EVANGELISM

"Then Philip went down to the city of Samaria, and preached Christ unto them. And the people with one accord gave heed unto those things which Philip spake, hearing and seeing the miracles which he did. For unclean spirits, crying with loud voice, came out of many that were possessed with them: and many taken with palsies, and that were lame, were healed."
Acts 8:5-7

Power evangelism has been a pattern in the New Testament since the beginning of the church. In these last days, a spirit of deception is blinding the eyes of the world. It takes an unction of the Holy Ghost on your life and ministry to break the power of that deception. Many unsaved people are bound by demonic spirits. Many times while witnessing, a spirit will speak to their mind while you are sharing your story. You must be able to discern the spirits and take authority over them right on the spot.

Just recently, I was taking to a lady that was unsaved. She came to a service because someone invited her, but struggled through the entire service. A demonic spirit was keeping her bound from coming to the altar and even trying to get her to leave the service. After the service I went to the back of the church and she was trying to leave. "Excuse me. How are you?" I asked. She looked at me with very empty eyes. "Not too good, even now," she replied. "Let me pray with you," I told her. As I began to pray, I received a word of knowledge and I broke a family curse off her life in the Name of Jesus. She fell to the floor in the foyer, shaking under the power of the Spirit. I quickly asked some ladies there to come pray with her. She got up a few minutes later. She looked at me and looked at the ladies and said, "I didn't think that stuff was real! Wow! I want to get saved!" We led her in the sinner's prayer and she received Jesus! That has happened so many times in the church and on the streets.

On Halloween night, in Greenville, South Carolina, I took evangelism teams downtown to the bars. One of our team members encountered a man wearing a vulgar and inappropriate costume and witnessed to him. God gave the team member a word of knowledge about the guy. He fell down under the power of conviction and ran home in shame that he was dressed like that and in public. Another team member prayed for a man and had a word of knowledge about an evil spirit. He took authority and broke the power of that spirit during the prayer of salvation. The man's eye was twitching, and his mouth was beginning to lock down so that he couldn't speak. The team member didn't get scared. He continued to take authority over the foul spirit. The man finished the prayer and fell out on the street. He got up set free and saved!

WNIM takes street ministry teams all over the nation, and we have seen numerous situations like these where the Holy Spirit is faithful to meet us right on the spot. He shows His power to meet the needs of the people we encounter.

Before you take teams out on the streets, or before you are going to witness, you should fast and pray. Ask God to release a fresh power of the Holy Spirit on you to be a witness and minister under clarity and effectiveness in the spirit realm. Repent of any known sin, and ask the Lord to convict you of any unknown sin also. Don't be in a rush to leave the prayer time. Wait on the Holy Spirit to endue you with the anointing!

When you are talking to someone, or praying with them, listen to the voice of the Holy Spirit. He will show you things by pictures and words of knowledge. Don't be afraid to ask questions to the person to investigate the leading of the Holy Spirit. When people first get saved or receive the baptism of the Holy Spirit, we have found that the Lord will often provide a heavy and clear prophetic direction for the person's life.

Step out on faith and see God work the miraculous through you. Lay hands on people and break the power of the enemy. Pray the prayer of salvation and always pray for a fresh unction and filling of the Holy Spirit in their life. I have had countless experiences like these that have changed peoples life's forever. God wants to use His people in power evangelism. Just step out there and do it. See the faithfulness of the Holy Spirit. I promise you, He won't leave you hanging.

THREE PHASES OF CORPORATE CHURCH EVANGELISM

Phase One: Grassroots Evangelism
"Now then we are ambassadors for Christ, as though God did beseech you by us: we pray you in Christ's stead, be ye reconciled to God."
2 Corinthians 5:20

All believers have been given a ministry of reconciliation. I believe with all my heart that if each Christian would simply tell their story of how Jesus touched them, there would be no need for an outreach department in the local church. The people become the outreach plan. God places His people around other people in the world who need deliverance from something they were set free from.

When I first got saved, I wasn't going to church. I was "burnt" by tradition and religion. I never wanted to go back to a traditional church again. I was really born again and full of the Spirit of the Lord. I was praying and reading my Bible at home, but didn't want any form of tradition in my life. I worked out everyday at the YMCA. There was this guy that came in to work out at the same time I did everyday. We just happened to do the same exercises on the same days. He was always talking about Jesus and he was always talking about his church. He kept inviting me to go and after years of hating organized religion, I found one that I connected with from day one. All it took was one invitation from someone who was really living for Jesus. One invite! After seeing he was real, I decided to break the vow I had made earlier to never set foot in a church again.

What is the number one reason people come to church? Because someone asked them to come! Yes, just because someone simply asked them to come to church, they agreed to come. The problem comes when we get too busy or embarrassed to ask our coworkers, friends, or family members if they are saved or if they will join us at church. The apostle Peter experienced pressure witnessing for Jesus. His life was threatened and he was thrown in jail. He had a great excuse not to share the gospel. But he didn't shut up or give up. Check out the example he gave to the entire church: *"And now, Lord, behold their threatenings: and grant unto thy servants, that with all boldness they may speak thy word." Acts 4:29*

Five thousand pastors leave the ministry each month. Why? The traditional role of reaching the lost has fallen on the pastor. Have you ever seen a shepherd give birth to a sheep? Sheep birth sheep. Shepherds watch over the sheep. A traditional church expects the pastor to do everything. That isn't a realistic expectation of a pastor. The people all around you may never hear your pastor, but they will listen to you. It's up to you to witness and be a light in those dark places.

I pastored a church for seven years. I believe it is essential for a pastor to teach a congregation to witness consistently and consistently invite people to church. When just a few people get a hold of it, your church will surge with new visitors. One day, at my church, a guy I knew from the club life before Christ, came in to the church and stayed for the service. At the end of the service he asked for prayer. Someone in his community had put a spell on him and he was scared. It was really messing him up. He had heard my testimony and knew I had come out of the occult. He wanted all the effects of the hex to be broken off him. I ask him, "Are you saved? Have you ever asked Jesus to forgive you of your sins and fill you with the Holy Spirit?" He replied, "No! I just want the spell taken off me." I told young man, "There is nothing I can do for you. You must be born again and receive Jesus Christ. Once His blood washed your sins, then the power of the curses can be broken." The guy looked at me with desperation and sincerity. "Man, I don't want to go to Hell and I sure don't want this mojo messin' me up. How do I get saved?"

I was able to lead this young man in the sinner's prayer. After that, I took authority over every demonic spell wrongfully working, by the power of the name of Jesus and the Blood of the Lamb. This young man fell on the ground shaking. He was on the ground saying, "Thank you Jesus! Thank you Jesus!" He got up and started to pray in the Spirit. He started to prophesy. He had a true encounter with Jesus. His girlfriend was with him and got saved, delivered and filled with the Spirit as well.

For the next few months, both never missed a service. They told everyone in their community about what God did for them. The first Sunday they came to church, they showed up with their parents. The next service they brought their cousins. Over the next six months, these guys brought everyone that would come with them to church. Just through their witness, the church grew by over hundred percent. It was amazing to what the power of two people, changed by the gospel, could do in a community. As a pastor, I quickly realized the value in training my members in basic evangelism skills. Jesus changed the entire world with twelve people. If I could get everyone in my church to be committed like those two, our church could easily change the city!

Corporate Evangelism Training

Salvation is a work of the Holy Spirit, and evangelism is the responsibility of the church. God certainly directs, anoints, and empowers, but the leadership of the local church is responsible to encourage and equip believers for evangelistic ministry. It is important to consistently teach your church the personal obligation they have to reach the lost. You must keep your teachings and exposures to the main church body short but consistent. Just as you would give a quick teaching about tithe before you take an offering up, or a quick teaching on baptisms, or communion, we have found that the same technique is effective concerning evangelism. Over time the concept will internalize corporately, eventually.

We recommend that every Sunday morning you fit in a five minute corporate teaching on evangelism. I have used all of these ideas:
- Short skits on Sunday morning on evangelism.
- Short videos on the necessity of evangelism. (www.sermoncentral.com)
- Consistent announcements of evangelistic events.
- Short five-minute teachings on personal evangelism.
- Evangelism classes on a consistent basis.

This is a card that we use to bring a simple, but effective teaching to the church. We have seen many people come to the Lord using this simple questions and approach.

Warrior Nations Street Ministry Strategy
✓ Do you know **God loves you** and has a **plan for your life**?

✓ If you died today, **would you go** to Heaven?

THE ROAD TO REDEMPTION:

1. ISN'T JUST BEING A MORALLY GOOD PERSON ENOUGH?
Romans 3:10 "As it is written, There is none righteous, no, not one.

2. AM I A SINNER?
Romans 3:23 "Yes, for all have sinned, and come short of the glory of God."

3. WHERE DID SIN COME FROM?
Romans 5:12 "Wherefore, as by one man sin entered into the world, and death passed upon all men, for that all have sinned."

4. GOD'S PRICE ON SIN.
Romans 6:23 "For the wages of sin is death, but the gift of God is eternal life through Jesus Christ our Lord."

5. OUR WAY OUT.
Romans 5:8 "But God commandeth His love toward us in that, while we were yet sinners, Christ died for us."

6. GOD SAYS.
Romans 10:9 "That if thou shalt confess with thy mouth the Lord Jesus, and shalt believe in thine heart that God raised Him from the death, thou shalt be saved.

7. YOU'RE A WHOSOEVER.
Romans 10:13 "For whosoever shall call upon the name of the Lord shall be saved."

Start praying for them and then ask them to join you. Pray the prayer of salvation with them.

CORPORATE CHURCH EVANGELISM

Phase Two: Evangelism Mobilization

Evangelism Mobilization is defined as a monthly outreach out from the church into the community.

"And he called unto them twelve, and began to send them forth by two and two; and gave them power over unclean spirits."
Mark 6:7-13

Jesus structured the New Testament church for growth. He gave us a pattern and then demonstrated that pattern for church growth. Everything Jesus did was on purpose. He knew He was setting the foundation for the Church. The Church in the New Testament went to the highways and the hedges. They didn't sit back in the "Box" of the four walls of the church, they went out and brought the Gospel to the people. Jesus gave us an awesome example of how we should go to the streets. He sent His evangelists out in pairs.

The first church that I ever pastored was in a part of town that was considered kind of rough by most of the community. I had been preparing for ministry three years and was launching my first outreach leading a church to conduct door-to-door evangelism. I preached about evangelism in the Sunday service and invited our thirty members to meet me next Saturday for the outreach. We just started the church plant and I was ready to take the block for Jesus. No one showed up for the outreach, so I made up my mind I was gonna go, lead some people to the Lord, bring some new convert to Sunday's service and tell everyone what the missed. I knocked on a few doors and no one came to the front. I would leave flyers about the church on the door and move on to the next house. After many empty efforts I finally had someone come to the door. A lady in house robe came to the door and opened her robe, flashed me and said, "Come on in pastor." I turned my head, back off the porch and took off down the street. I am walking down the road and told God, "I didn't expect that." The Holy Spirit replied, "You know that part of scripture where it says and they went out two by two?" I said, "Yes Lord." He said, "That's why!"

Why are the fastest growing religions in the world out growing the local church in North America? The Mormon Church has a plan. They go out, two by two. They asked every young person to commit two years of their life to go on a mission. There they go away from home and go from door to door passing out pamphlets and telling people about the Latter Day Saints church. While I strongly disagree with their theology, I can see why they do have a massive growth curve over the past few decades. There have structured their pattern of outreach, like Jesus and given two years of their life to their version of evangelism. What if the people in your church gave the same commitment to evangelism that the LDS does?

If your church isn't following the New Testament model for growth, it simply won't grow. Ninety percent of North American churches have fewer than one hundred members. Why is that? A lot of factors contribute to that statistic, but I believe the number one factor is a failure to employ God's pattern for growth. A church that is not evangelizing is fossilizing. Every church is different and might use different methods of evangelism, but the ones that are doing something are the one that are growing. No matter what method your church uses, the message should remain the same. God loves people and has an awesome plan for them. There is a church that wants to help them fulfill God's plan. Hell is real, but God doesn't want them there! He sent His Son to pay the price for their sin.

Here are several examples of monthly outreaches to your community. Invite people to come and then witness to them.

- Establish a Food Bank or open up a Thrift Store
- Take inventory of the business owners who are a part of your church and organize an event to provide free or discounted services to the needy (vehicle maintenance, hair care, etc.)
- Unemployment Workshops
- Monthly Youth-Led Church Services
- Marketplace Ministry Fairs
- Monthly Church Meals Inviting Guests (Churches that do this have a 70% retention rate of their members.)
- Sports Night/UFC Fight Night, Football, Basketball, Soccer
- Wild Game Dinners/"You Kill 'em, We Grill 'em" Nights
- Door-to-Door Visitation to the Surrounding Community.
- Going to Local Events, or Busy Areas and Witness. Pass Out Info About Your Church. Football Games, Malls, Retail Stores, Carnivals, etc.
- Movie Night and Invite a Friend.

CORPORATE CHURCH EVANGELISM

Phase Three: 90 Day Special Events

Phase one and two support phase three. Many churches use phase three as their main or only form of evangelism, which is the very order of evangelism the church needs to rethink.

Nick Hill is a pastor in Kingston, Tennessee. His church is surrounded by lower income houses and apartments. He has been reaching out to the people of his community for years. He has such a heart to see change for his city. The city has about 13,000 people. One day, a man from the community around the church got mad because someone was changed by the power of Jesus that was close to him. He came in and tried to burn the church down. That was horrible, but it didn't stop the church from reaching out to the surrounding people. Nick put on his church sign, "Prostitutes, Drug Addicts and Alcoholics Welcome Here." All of the sudden, people were coming in that were fitting that description and getting saved!

He was starting to see a slow, but steady impact in the area. One day the Holy Spirit prompted him to have a "Battle of the Bands" in the city park, next to the church. He didn't make it Christian bands only, but made it a city-wide event. He ask the bands that did participate to sign an agreement that there would be no inappropriate content in their songs. The church started to go out two by two and pass out flyers about the event. The got a chance to witness to many people in the town that would never just show up at church. Nearly the entire town was buzzing about this concert! On the day of the event pastor Nick put a baptismal pool by the stage and asked his church members to bring a towels. By faith, his church believed they would lead many to the Lord. As the day went on, hundreds and hundreds of people showed up and flocked to the concert. Nick looked up and saw the field was covered with people. He said, "Where in the world did all these people come from?" Close to 2,000 people came for the concert and they led many in the sinner's prayer and baptized them on the spot.

I was with one of the evangelist for, Winter Jam, one of the most enduring and successful Christian music concert series in North America. Tony Nolan has been the main evangelist on this outreach for many years. Tony and I have a mutual friend who lives down the street from him. We met a few years ago, and my wife and I were able to go back stage during the event in Greenville, South Carolina. Tony took me to the soundboard and explained all the sound equipment they were using. He showed me a lot of technical things back stage and told me all the extensive details that it took to put on the event. During the altar time, Tony used text messages to get the follow up information during the event, because there might be ten to fifteen thousand people in the stadiums. Back in his dressing room, Tony has a computer set up to get all the information after it is sent in. Once he is able to view and pray over the decisions, he can email all the names to the area pastors for follow up.

Every stop on the Winter Jam tour has a very powerful impact in the regions where they are held. Each idea is targeted and has different dynamics. Each leader has to see the value in these ideas and methods. You know your area and your people better than a visitor. At all three levels of this church evangelism strategy you will know which ideas your people will receive and which will best work for you. Pick a method that works, but don't change the message!

Why is the "traditional role" of an Evangelist still important to the local church? When a church is expecting a guest speaker, there is a necessary expectation that isn't normally taking place at your average service.

Here are some outreach ideas that create expectation:
- Special Speakers
- Holiday Outreaches
- Concerts & Worship Events
- Summer Revivals
- Beyond the Darkness Exposés
- Back to School Rallies
- World Harvest Crusades (Mission Trips)

KINGDOM SYNERGY

"For as the body is one, and hath many members, and all the members of that one body, being many, are one body: so also is Christ. For by one Spirit are we all baptized into one body, whether we be Jews or Gentiles, whether we be bond or free; and have been all made to drink into one Spirit. For the body is not one member, but many. If the foot shall say, Because I am not the hand, I am not of the body; is it therefore not of the body? And if the ear shall say, Because I am not the eye, I am not of the body; is it therefore not of the body? If the whole body were an eye, where were the hearing? If the whole were hearing, where were the smelling? But now hath God set the members every one of them in the body, as it hath pleased him. And if they were all one member, where were the body? But now are they many members, yet but one body."
1 Corinthians 12:12-20

The World English Dictionary defines "synergism" as "the potential ability of individual organizations or groups to be more successful or productive as a result of a merger."

"Synergy is the creation of a whole that is greater than the sum of its parts" (Ray French, Charlotte Rayner, Gary Rees, Sally Rumbles, *Organizational Behaviours.*).

Jesus never meant for the Church to be a one man show. One strength of many fast growing ministries is that the leaders learned to disciple and release people into their function of ministry. I am very aware, as a leader, that the worst thing to do is release someone into a place before they are ready, but the worst thing a leader can do is never release them, or delay in their release.

I was doing an interview in Dallas, TX at the main Daystar Television Network, with Marcus and Joni Lamb. I had been asked to come out for a five-part series on the spirit realm, with John Paul Jackson giving spiritual symbolism on my testimony and what happens to many people in the spirit realm when coming out of situations like mine.

While I was traveling to the network the Holy Spirit spoke to me and said, "You are going to have an opportunity to ask questions to someone who has had uncommon impact in my Kingdom." I thought to myself, "Ok, Lord!" When I arrived I met a man from Lagos, Nigeria named Bishop Matthew Ashimolowo. He has started a church ten years ago in London, England and it now has become the largest church in the United Kingdom. During that time he has had over 1,000 satellite churches planted under the name, "Kingsway Christian International Church."

I sat on set directly beside Bishop Matthew. All of his and my associates left the room for a moment. We had several minutes before we were going to be interviewed. I ask him, "What happened to cause your churches to grow so fast?" He replied, "The grace of the Lord Jesus Christ." I said, "Yes, I understand that is the only thing, but what did that look like?' He looked at me surprised that I was pulling this out of him right before a worldwide TV interview, but I remembered what the Holy Spirit said to me and I might never have a moment like this again, so I went for it. He said, "I disciple my people, saw the callings, helped them in it, and then released them into it. The more I gave away and delegated liberty and authority to go and do ministry, the faster it grew. I have never forgotten this kingdom synergy revelation he spoke to me that day.

"And he gave some, apostles; and some, prophets; and some, evangelists; and some, pastors and teachers; For the perfecting of the saints, for the work of the ministry, for the edifying of the body of Christ. Till we all come in the unity of the faith, and of the knowledge of the Son of God, unto a perfect man, unto the measure of the stature of the fullness of Christ."
Ephesians 4:11-13 KJV

I have worked with many men and women of God over the years and been in some "Azusa" type services that have been a direct result of unity and harmony of the five-fold ministry gifts working together without competition or strife. I think that the key to lasting revival in a church is only going to be found in the pure working together of the saints and leaders. Not motivated by selfish ambitions, or impure motives, but to advance Christ's Kingdom agenda alone. I've seen authentic moves of the Holy Spirit quenched by people who were more worried about whose name were on the flyer, or who was going to get the offering that night. I've learned that God has commanded His blessing in the place of unity and that's where I want to be.

In these last days, more and more ministries must work together in order to complete the Great Commission. We must put aside our denomination differences and work together to bring in the last great harvest of souls before Jesus Christ's second coming. It takes a city to take a city, and it takes a region to take a region. If any man or ministry thinks he can do it alone, he is in trouble.

I was in Beverly Hills, California preaching a series of meetings and doing TV interviews. I was driving through the city and had a vision of a huge stage with little faces all in the floor of the platform. It looked like they were clear coated in the platform. Where the pulpit should have been, I saw three spears all pointing up toward heaven. As I looked closer, I saw the faces of the fathers of the faith over the past. I saw faces from all denominations and groups. I saw Oral Roberts, Kenneth Hagin, Adrian Rodgers, William Seymour, and oh so many more. I asked the Lord what that meant. He said that what I saw was a foundation of teaching and revelation that this current generation had benefited from. This new generation would be different in the sense that they are standing on that platform, but they would be a nameless and faceless generation. The spears represented the Trinity working in this generation in an uncommon level of unity.

As I have been working in churches across America to implement this evangelism concept, I recommend that you implement all three phases for a minimum of at least one year. It takes many impressions of the teachings and process for your church to get a rhythm and find what works for your church and your community. It, also, takes all of these functions happening at the same time to really build a momentum that shifts your rate of growth. We find that a year is a common amount of time that it takes for the church to internalize the teachings. They become more automatic, rather than just another program. There is a Latin Proverb that says, "Repetition is the mother of learning."

THE OFFICE OF AN EVANGELIST

What does the office of the evangelist in the local church look like? For many years, the understanding of the evangelist in the North American church has been the one of having a special speaker on certain times of the year, that has the gift of evangelism, to do outreach. We invite our friends and family to the church during this time and see many people come to the saving knowledge of Christ. This is a powerful dynamic of evangelism that has been very effective for the church. During the Billy Graham era, "event evangelism" birthed a whole new dynamic for the Body. Masses have been saved through setting up concerts with popular musicians and talent designed to get worldly people to come to "churchy" events. This has set a standard in North American mass outreach in many arenas.

While many of these events are planned and organized by someone who operates in the *office* of an evangelist, that is not the main role of the office of an evangelist.

Ephesians 4:11-12, "And he gave some, apostles; and some, prophets; and some, evangelists; and some, pastors and teachers; For the perfecting (equipping) of the saints, for the work of the ministry, for the edifying of the body of Christ:"

The word "Evangelist" in this scripture in the Greek root means, "to announce good news ("evangelize") especially the gospel: - declare, bring (declare, show) glad (good) tidings, preach (the gospel)." The word "equipping" in Greek means "aligning" like a chiropractor aligning a back.

The role of the office, at its core, is to preach the message of Christ and to train the evangelist in the local church in this gift and then mobilize them of all type of evangelistic events. You might think of it as an in-house evangelist, or outreach pastor. They can step into the pulpit to preach also, if needed. There is an anointing on them to see people saved, but they aren't in the pulpit all the time and their focus is on taking the Gospel message to the community.

The role of the visiting or interactive evangelist is very important because people have an expectation at special events that they do not normally have at an average weekly service. However, it becomes a problem when this is the only evangelism function in your church. In that case, there is a huge void in the responsibility of the local church to outreach. A senior pastor/overseer/apostle can't carry the evangelism of the community. If he tries, the five-fold function will be dysfunctional.

Evangelists shouldn't try to pastor and pastors shouldn't try to be an evangelist! Everyone should stay in their own calling and work together. That kind of unity creates a maximizing impact that couldn't happen if jealousy and envy keep the gifts competing against each other and building their own empires, instead of Christ's kingdom.

I believe in the function of all five gifts working together to perfect the local church. It is in this synergistic relationship that I have described the role of the evangelist. The apostle/senior pastor is the "sent one" that has the vision for the church. The prophet/head intercessor is the one that has special divine direction to confirm or clarify the vision. Both the apostle and prophet work close together. Prayer warriors, intercessors, and prayer ministries are usually under the office of a prophet.

The true pastoral role is one that visits new members, visits the hospitalized, checks on those who haven't been at church in a while, conducts marriage counseling, etc. The office of a pastor is one that usually is over the functions like these. He is also one who trains and mobilizes the pastors. The office of a teacher's role is one that is over the training classes of the main Body. He is mobilizing the new member's classes and preparing special teachings for each age range and need in the local church. He is over the rotations of these functions.

You shouldn't build the church on one of these functions alone. If your church isn't balanced in these giftings, your church will be dysfunctional! The more balanced the functions are in the church, the stronger the church will be. For example, look at how a team of musicians work together and a rule they must abide by, in order to flow together effectively.

Rule of One *"If you are the only instrument, you cover everything but the melody (unless it's an instrumental section), so you play chords, harmony, groove etc. As you add more instruments you should play less to give each other a space for their part. So if there are five people in the band then you should play a fifth of the time."* There will be times when you will have solos, but the harmony comes from the unity.

I believe that this is a picture of God's perfect function for the New Testament church, but it looks different for every church and should be based on the church's mission and needs. When you look at the Ephesians 4 model in Scripture, we see the need for these functions.

Ephesians 4:11-12, "And he gave some, apostles; and some, prophets; and some, evangelists; and some, pastors and teachers; For the perfecting (equipping) of the saints, for the work of the ministry, for the edifying of the body of Christ:"

Bishop Dale Bonner from Austell, Georgia started a church with a leadership model like this. He saw his church start with a few hundred and exploded to over 10,000 members in a few short years. He tells a story of walking up to a vending machine one day and putting some change into it. He tapped the button to receive his selection and then noticed the sign on the machine that said, "Out of Order."

He said the Holy Spirit whispered something to him that would forever change his life. "Never invest in anything that is out of order!" A church that doesn't have the function of the five-fold ministry operating in its' house is simply out of order. It doesn't mean that they aren't called or doing a good work, but it does mean that it will not function correctly until all the dynamics get in order. A church might not call each office an apostle, prophet, teacher, pastor, or evangelist, but the function of that office should be well in operation.

One thing I have found out trying to establish this model in several churches is that you have to build the concept around the function of the gift, not a person with the gift in that office. Anytime a man in an office is lifted up, it can be dangerous. Jesus will not share His glory with any man and a function taught to many is harder to stop than a man operating in a function alone.

THE SECRET TO EVANGELISM

My very first city-wide evangelism meeting was the biggest lesson the Holy Spirit ever gave me on the secret to evangelism. I'll never forget the night. I had been campaigning for two months in the city with a handful of church leaders. I prepared commercials, flyers, counselor training, and newspaper. I had followed all the things on my evangelism plan list and checked them twice. I was fasting so much that I looked bad. My eyes had dark circles under them and I was beat from no sleep praying and no energy for fasting. I had done all the things in *Evangelism 101*. It was the big night and I was praying to God for the entire city to be saved. I had rented the local high school gym and had some locally known musicians there for worship. It was a great time of worship and a powerful message. We had a good crowd attend and it got down to the altar call. I gave the call with all the passion I had. As I looked over the auditorium, I saw hundreds of people. Not one of them moved! Not one person responded!

I dismissed the service and ran behind the stage curtain where no one could hear or see me. I stood there in shock, as to what just happened. I didn't want to see anyone, or talk to anyone. I just wanted God to tell me what in the world just happened. "God, why didn't people respond to the message? What's the deal? What did I do wrong?" I never forget the words the Holy Spirit burned into my heart that night. He said to me, "You don't produce the anointing, the anointing produces you! The secret to preaching the Gospel is simply preaching the Gospel."

No matter how dynamic your desire to evangelize, you should always keep this one thing in mind. Methodology might change, but the message should never change. Faith in the message should supersede faith in the methodology. I believe that having a good core strategy for outreach is essential for any ministry that wants to impact their city. The Bible says in James that "Faith without works is dead". No matter what your strategy is, it should have the heart of Jesus Christ at its' core. Don't do it because you want the biggest church, or ministry in town. Do it because you have a passion to see people changed for His glory and by His Spirit. When you get to this point, God will take your natural plans and put His supernatural anointing on them.

Mother Teresa was one of the greatest influences for the Gospel in the twentieth century, and, certainly by all standards, she was a powerful of evangelist of the Gospel. She was able to touch the world with her passion and inspire many to become a carrier of the torch of Christ.

She was asked one day what was the secret to becoming such a mighty success for the Kingdom of Christ. She looked at the questioner without delay and responded: *"I never look at the masses as my responsibility; I look at the individual. I can only love one person at a time - just one, one, one. So you begin. I began - I picked up one person. Maybe if I didn't pick up that one person, I wouldn't have picked up forty-two thousand....The same thing goes for you, the same thing in your family, the same thing in your church, your community. Just begin - one, one, one."*

APPENDIX

Event Promotional Tools and Materials

A Note To The Host Church: This letter has been of the greatest tools in creating excitement in your community among other area churches. Please type this letter up on your church letterhead, make copies, and send it to as many churches in your area as possible. Send to all churches. We are sure the response will astound you. Through the mailing of this letter we have seen many churches of different denominations become a part of Shawn Patrick's Exposés. Please use the promotional material that we have provided for you. Make copies. Be creative. We have found that the use of this letter together with a poster and a bio sketch, etc. will be some of the most effective, lowest cost, advertising you can do for the Exposé.

Sample Letter For Promotional Use

Dear Pastor,

Greetings in the lovely name of our Lord and Savior Jesus Christ! The days of (date of Exposé) could be significant ones for the young people and parents of your Church.

It is the night that we will be presenting the ministry of Evangelist Shawn Patrick Williams from Greenwood, South Carolina here in our (Church, Auditorium, etc.) in (City, State). Rev. Williams is well known for his presentation of "Beyond the Darkness: Exposing Occultism In America." Shawn Patrick deals with the hard-hitting, sometimes controversial issues of our day. During the 3 or 4 night Exposé, Shawn Patrick will be presenting the shocking evidence of rock and rap music's influences on our culture. This former drug dealer and bar owner will share with you his unique insight into today's rock and rap culture with all its sexual perversion, violence, and occult themes! Please be assured that Shawn Patrick's ministry is not just another "Occult Talk" but a multi-media event that will have a profound effect upon our churches and our community for years to come.

"Beyond the Darkness" is undoubtedly a very respected and a highly recommended contemporary ministry. Shawn Patrick has, through years of research and actual involvement in the world of music and the occult, become one of this nation's foremost Christian authorities in this area. Enclosed you'll find personal information on Rev. Williams, including recommendations of his ministry from various pastors and community leaders plus media for display in your church as well as some bulletin inserts. Please feel free to reproduce any of this material to help promote this Exposé among your people.

(The following paragraph is optional and may be excluded if you feel that your Church can provide an adequate number of Counselors and Ushers.)

We want to provide you and your Associate Pastor or Youth Pastor an opportunity of meeting personally with Bro. Williams and his family as he conducts a C.U.P.P. (Counselors, Ushers, Pastors, and Prayer Warriors) orientation meeting. This will be held at our church (or other location) on Saturday night (date) at (time) prior to the Exposé which begins Sunday night (date). Please come with your wife and also invite as many as possible committed couples from your church to serve as counselors. Everyone involved with the Exposé will be briefed and trained this night. Bro. Williams will be providing all counseling material. Just bring a pen, note pad, and your

Bible. Please know that your attendance is crucial to the success of this community wide Exposé.

The (your church name) is underwriting the cost of this Exposé in cooperation with Shawn Patrick and his Exposé team expenses during the Exposé. A freewill love-offering will be received each night with all proceeds going to Warrior Nations International Ministries. Shawn Patrick has not asked for any type of financial guarantees. He is coming by faith, believing God that the needs of his ministry will be met.

We ask you to prayerfully consider the information provided and we hope that you will accept our invitation for your church to come and be a part of what God is doing in our midst through this dynamic ministry. We believe that reaching LOST SOULS of men and women, young and old, is the primary objective of each church we are contacting. We prayerfully ask you and your church to participate in this revival. We also hope that you will help us in following up on the great harvest that we are anticipating. We will be directing all those who make decisions to the church of their preference. We also encourage you to run your church bus or van each night. Please give us a call at least one week in advance so that we may reserve a seat for your group. We are very excited about the upcoming "Beyond the Darkness" family Exposé with Evangelist

Shawn Patrick Williams and are looking forward to working together with you and your church as we lift up Jesus to those who are lost and dying in our community. I know that once you have experienced Shawn Patrick's "Beyond the Darkness" your life nor the lives of your church will ever be the same again! If you have any questions, need directions, or need additional information, please do not hesitate to call, our office number is (Add your office telephone number).

Yours In Christ,
Pastor

Pre-Event Checklist

Check each item when completed….
- o Thoroughly read and understand "How to Plan A Successful Event" brochure.
- o The best date, place, time, have been selected for optimum results during the event?
- o Have all materials been received? ___Church Promo Packets, ___ Counselors Material, ___Promo Video, ___CUPP Video.
- o Publicity is the most vital part of having good attendance. Please make sure that every step has been taken to assure proper publicity and promotion.
- o Radio…(using our Radio Spots? Interviews?) Consider buying air time.
- o Newspaper…(Ads? Interviews? Reprints?) We would be happy to arrange a phone interview between Brother Shawn Patrick and the local press prior to his arrival. (Please call our office to arrange). Use all Stations, Radio, TV, and all Newspapers.
- o Television…(Using our Spots? Interviews? Try community cable, it's very inexpensive.)
- o Posters and Flyers distributed? How many?_____
Where?_____
- o Letters sent to area churches?_____
Response?_____
- o Promo T-Shirts given away?____To whom?_____
- o Christian bookstores contacted? Offering discount?_____
- o Phone calls to area Pastors? Response?____Follow-Up?____
- o Youth groups committed to come?_____Sunday night is the best night!
- o Inserts included in church bulletins?

Three weeks prior to Exposé.
- o High School Info. Pack received? _____Video? ____Assemblies Schedules?
- o Signs, billboards, etc?___ Where?_____
Try banks, other church marquees.
- o Please send itinerary to our office by _____(3 weeks prior to Exposé dates) Please include a map and directions.
- o Thoroughly read and understand "Suggested Event Format"

brochure.
- Prayer envelopes are to be placed on pews. The offering received in the middle of the service is not an intermission. It can hinder the altar times if done at the end of the service.
- Altar call music?_____
- Music? Special Music slated? Please be sure they are ANOINTED, CONTEMPRARY, musicians. Make certain Shawn Patrick is introduced before or no later than 7:20 pm each night. Our 30-minute Pre-Exposé CD will play from 6:30-7:00.
- Thoroughly read and understand "Required Set-Up Material" brochure.
- Set up church (please have three people available to help unload the equipment- be sure all buildings are accessible.
- Two eight-foot tables for use with ministry table in a good location (FOYER IS BEST).
- Select the best counseling area.
- Are there backup rooms in case of overflow response?_____ Closed circuit TV?_____
- If Event is held at location other than the church, please review the 14 additional steps for a large Exposé.
- C.U.P.P. Video & Promo Video to be viewed BEFORE the Event.
- Counselors, Ushers, Pastors, and Prayer Warriors meeting scheduled for Saturday evening at 7:00 PM.
- Number of people at video showing?_____ Total # of Counselors?_____
- Promo Video shown? (Sun. or Wed. night prior to crusade).
- Head Counselors selected for men and women?_____
- Parking Attendants?_____
- Nursery?_____ A MUST!!! Need qualified attendants. Consider having a snack and drink provided for children due to the time of services.
- Please make these arrangements well in advance of the Event. ___Accommodations? ___Meals?

*Signature*_____
Completed & Signed by: _____
*Position/Tile:*_____*Date:*_____

Special Events Counselors Training and Support Materials

ISN'T JUST BEING A MORALLY GOOD PERSON ENOUGH?
ROMANS 3:10 As it is written, There is none righteous, no, not one.

AM I A SINNER?
ROMANS 3:23 Yes, For all have sinned, and come short of the glory of God.

WHERE DID SIN COME FROM?
ROMANS 5:12 Wherefore, as by one man sin entered into the world, and death passed upon all men, for that all have sinned.

GOD'S PRICE ON SIN.
ROMANS 6:23 For the wages of sin is death, but the gift of God is eternal life through Jesus Christ our Lord.

OUR WAY OUT.
ROMANS 5:8 But God commendeth His love toward us in that, while we were yet sinners, Christ died for us.

GOD SAYS.
ROMANS 10:9 That if thou shalt confess with thy mouth the Lord Jesus, and shalt believe in thine heart that God hath raised Him from the dead, thou shalt be saved.

YOU'RE A "WHOSOEVER."
ROMANS 10:13 For whosoever shall call upon the name of the Lord shall be saved.

WILL YOU CALL UPON THE LORD NOW, AND ASK HIM TO SAVE YOU?

Then, pray this prayer now.... "Dear God, I confess that I am a sinner, I am sorry for my sin, and I ask you for mercy and forgiveness through the blood of your Son, Jesus. I believe He died for me and rose again. I now accept Him as my Savior!
--CONGRATULATIONS!--
Friend, if you just prayed that prayer, and meant it from the heart you have just become a new member of the Kingdom of God. "A new

creature" old things are passed away; behold, all things are become new. 2 Corinthians 5:17.

Now God expects you to grow in your new found faith. How? By communicating with God daily thru prayer, by reading His Word, the Bible daily, by witnessing for Him, telling others what He has done in your life, by fellowshipping with other believers in a Bible believing, Bible teaching church, and by following Jesus' example of Baptism. We here at Warrior Nations love you and are praying with you. Please take a few minutes to write us a letter of testimony so that we may rejoice with you in what God has done in your life. Remember God loves you and I'm excited about what He has in store for you!
Shawn Patrick & Christy Williams

Counselor's Check-Off List

You are important!
- Begin with short PRAYER
- Counselors fill out COMMITMENT CARD
- Go over questions & scriptures on ROAD TO REDEMPTION
- Counselor acknowledge commitment of counselee- if first time profession of faith then….WELCOME TO FAMILY (OF GOD)
- Give salvation booklet to each new First-Time Believer- Give ROAD TO REDEMPTION & 7 STEPS TO VICTORIOUS WARFARE to each counselee no matter what their decision.
- Have counselee LOOK UP SCRIPTURES at home.
- Ask counselee to INVITE TWO FRIENDS to come to the Exposé the next night.
- CLOSE WITH PRAYER.
- WRITE NOTE OF ENCOURAGEMENT to each counselee.
- GIVE CARDS & NOTES TO HEAD COUNSELORS or place in drop box on table

Counselor's Information

1) Be at the auditorium by 6:30 PM nightly.
2) Pray for at least 20 minutes prior to the meeting.

3) Be alert for the altar call.
4) When people start going forward, you go forward as well.
5) At the altar:
6) Let them know you love them.
7) Male with male, female with female.
8) Be alert when head counselor asks you to go in the separate room.
9) Counseling/ Soul-winning
10) Deal collectively (if you have several people)
11) Avoid heavy theological discussions.
12) If you have a problem, call the head counselor.
13) Fill out the commitment card: (Please make sure the counselor completes the information)
- Your name
- Counselee's name
- Counselee's age
- Address and phone number
- Church affiliation
- What did they specifically come for?
- Important! Do you want a pastor to call? Put extenuating circumstances on the back of the card.
14) Use the Roman's Road scriptures. (Road to Redemption handout)
15) Two questions to ask to ensure if they are saved:
- "If you died tonight, would you go to heaven?"
- "If you died and stood before Jesus and he asked why he should allow you into Heaven, what would you answer?"

If there are any questions regarding this material, please feel free to call the office.

A Call to Prayer C.U.P.P Meeting

- Unity among Pastors/ Leadership
- Motivation of Christians to participate, pray, and work
- The needs of Warrior Nations International Ministries, Inc. and this Exposé to be met.
- Health, strength, anointing on Bro. Shawn Patrick, staff, and all Exposé workers
- Effective time of ministry at schools and Exposé services
- Conviction of the Holy Spirit to repentance and salvation

- Effective and anointed music ministry
- Quality follow-up
- Participating churches will continue to bring people to Jesus and will nurture the new converts to maturity in their walk with Christ.

7 Steps for Victorious Warfare

Please know that Christianity is not a 100-yard dash. It is an endurance run!

1) Beginning tomorrow morning set your alarm clock 15 minutes early.
2) Begin each day in praise and prayer to the Lord (Remember prayer is not a monologue, prayer is a dialogue).
3) Read the Word daily. Remember that the spirit man eats only Bible food.
4) This Sunday find a Bible-believing church where the Lord is honored and attend faithfully.
5) Be baptized as an outward expression of an inward change of heart.
6) Tell your friends the good news.
7) Go through your belongings and get rid of anything ungodly (such as music, clothing, posters, occult jewelry, books, etc.).
8) Tune in to Christian radio and television.

Need a little more? Would you like help implementing <u>Rethinking Evangelism: Outside the Box</u> book information in your church?

Have Shawn Patrick come to your church, train, and work with your leaders to implement this 12-month outreach plan. Call the WNIM office in Greenwood, South Carolina for more information at 864-227-0508. You may also visit us online at <u>warriornations.org</u> and send a request at info@warriornations.org.

Shawn Patrick Williams

Looking for like-minded fellowship? Do you or your ministry need a spiritual covering? Want to be a part of a ministry community? Take a look at our fellowship.

Vision Statement

Warrior Nations Fellowship is a cross-generational, cross-cultural ministerial fellowship that extends all national, international, and socioeconomic lines. We have a passion for God's kingdom, family, community and the end time harvest. It is our desire for each member to know who they are in Christ based on God's Word, what their authority is in the kingdom of God, and how to operate in our culture through the principles of God's Word. Warrior Nations Fellowship believes that the Christian life is a life of faith and integrity.

Warrior Nations Fellowship has a vision to recognize, develop, and release ministries into the body of Christ. We acknowledge the apostle, prophet, teacher, pastor and evangelist as current, functioning offices in the government of the Church. We believe all gifts are equally needed in the Body to work in harmony with each other to fully equip the saints. Warrior Nations International Fellowship believes every Christian has a "place" in the body of Christ and we purpose to help and assist each believer to find that "place."

We believe as each ministry understands who they are according to God's Word, that they will find their place in the Body of Christ. As these ministries and believers are released back into the communities and nations, we will see God restore His Church back into the New Testament function in which it was created to function.

www.warriornations.org/warrior-nations-fellowship

Shawn Patrick Williams

ABOUT THE AUTHOR

After being radically saved from 10 years of drug and occult involvement in a bar through a Damascus road experience, Shawn Patrick received a burning commission to evangelize the United States and the world. His style of preaching brings a revival culture to the Body of Christ. He attended Christ Life School of Theology and received his Masters in Psychology from the Institute of Theology and Christian Therapy in Granbury, Texas.

Recognized nationally and internationally as a man of God, Shawn Patrick passionately speaks each year through radio, TV, conferences, festivals, concerts, and in over twenty-five different denominations. He has a Doctor of Divinity from Dayspring University and was ordained as a bishop in 2009. He then launched Warrior Nations Fellowship, which is an association for ministers and ministries. Shawn Patrick lives in Greenwood, South Carolina with his wife Christy and their four children: Sethe Patrick, Isabella Jordan, Ada Grace, and John Ellison.

Made in the USA
Charleston, SC
01 March 2015